Sportswear
in
VOGUE

Sportswear
in
VOGUE

SINCE 1910

by Charlie Lee-Potter

ABBEVILLE PRESS · PUBLISHERS · NEW YORK

ACKNOWLEDGMENTS

I am indebted to Alex Kroll, Editor of Condé Nast Books, for his encouragement and good humor, and to Liz Prior and Elizabeth Wickham for their untiring work on the book's design. My thanks are also extended to Bunny Cantor, the Condé Nast librarian, and to Patrick Handley and Timothy Hyde for their help with the chores. Most of all, I am grateful to Christina Probert for her invaluable editorial work and her expert and patient "answering service" to all my questions.

C.L.-P

To my mother

Library of Congress Cataloging in Publication Data

Lee-Potter, Charlie.
Sportswear in Vogue since 1910.

1. Sport clothes for women—History—20th century.
2. Vogue—History—20th century. 3. Sports for women—
History—20th century. I. Vogue. II. Title.
GT1855.L45 1984   391'.8   83-26574
ISBN 0-89659-499-8

Cover. BV 1983 Patrick Demarchelier. *Zoran.*
Back cover. BV 1923 Ann Fish. Page 2. IV 1980 Barry Lategan. *Rocco Barocco.*

CONTENTS

Key to captions

Information is given in the following order: edition; artist or photographer; designer or maker (the last always in *italic*). Editions are identified by initials:

A V American *Vogue*
B V British *Vogue*
F V French *Vogue*
G V German *Vogue*
I V Italian *Vogue*

INTRODUCTION

'Half the fun of sports – or is it really all the fun? –
lies in wearing just the smartest type of sports clothes.'
(American *Vogue*, 1919.)

In 1910 sport for women was a dressing-up game; convention had everything to do with the development of the sporting mode and practicality relatively little. 'Since men are the creators of sports clothes, they may consistently claim to be the arbiters of questions as to the right and wrong way to wear them', said *Vogue*. For the first years of this century women were hampered by a desire to emulate men in their sports dress. Little credit was given to Christina Willes who, because the width of her skirt prevented her adopting the traditional underarm style, pioneered overarm bowling in cricket in the early 1800s. Most sports were initially characterized by restrictive clothing, but 'Society's motor maids', revelling in an exhilarating sport which did not require them to wear impossibly stifling clothes, were eager to sport the latest fashions, such as moiré-lined catskin coats or double-breasted camel hair coats with detachable leather linings. Once again they were anxious to imitate and be approved by men, adopting their rubber slipover shirts with elastic cuffs, and even borrowing their brilliantine to keep their hair in place.

The 'Rational Dress Society', founded in 1881, pioneered the wearing of trousers for sport, emulating Mrs Amelia Jenks Bloomer who, in the early nineteenth century, had originated for daytime wear what was effectively the first trouser suit for women. The long loose trousers she wore beneath her knee-length dresses were developed further in the early twentieth century by Poiret and Chanel. Towelling 'Oxford Bags', originally worn by Oxford undergraduates in the mid twenties over their rowing shorts, were later adopted by women as chic day and sportswear.

As long as women in sport were treated derisorily, *Vogue* tended to picture them holding racquets and clubs in limp hands and wearing their everyday clothes. The decade's straight skirts were not specially adapted, other than by the insertion of box pleats from the knee downwards; but even the value of these was negated by the puritanical tendency to stitch them down. Competitiveness was not encouraged, and so clothes which enabled women to win were not necessary. Golfers were permitted expanding pleats on either side of the back of the jacket, to allow for 'the longest drive', but other sports did not fare so well. Even specific gloves were advised for

Bare arms and bound heads make up the tennis look in the twenties.
BV 1927 Harriet Meserole

1910

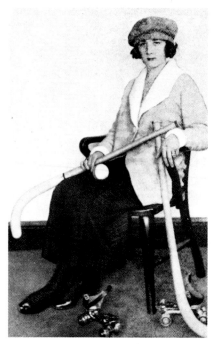

This sedentary sportswoman intends to play hockey and skate in her smart yellow woollen coat. BV 1919

One of the first examples of an aviator's hat, this tan hide, felt-lined helmet features a detachable extension rim to protect the head in case of accident. AV 1911

walking: 'the heavy English hand sewn walking glove'.

Fashion was following very different paths in Europe and America. In America sportswear developed much more freely, unhampered as it was by established craftsmanship traditions, and, unlike the Europeans, the Americans came out of the First World War richer than they had been before. Consequently, they took the lead: hemlines were shorter, astride riding more common and a swifter development in the ready-to-wear industry made more clothes available.

The tango originated in America in 1911 and swept across the western world: 'So violent is the tango madness that even skaters, denied the actual dance, console themselves with its garb – a black velvet skirt with slash and pleated chiffon insert.' To add a note of sobriety absent from the dance floor, snap fasteners were inserted along the pleat so that it could be kept shut during repose. The early years of the decade had seen Poiret's attempts to free the waistline, but only at the expense of the legs, which he 'shackled'; following the lead of mainstream fashion, however, skaters were released from these imprisoning skirts by mid-decade. By 1919 holidays abroad were possible again and skiing and skating were eagerly practised. The oriental influence, prevalent since the Ballets Russes' first performance in Paris in 1909, continued, and skating outfits were its chief sporting manifestation. Persian patterned pongee silk skating blouses with matching draw-string bags at the wrist were coveted by all; an orgy of fur – stoles, muffs and hats – completed the Russian look. Skirts trimmed with heavy bands of fur round the hem to weigh them down and prevent an immodest display of the legs were smart too, especially when they were accentuated by brilliant ethnic sashes round the waist. For skiing, long, slit skirts over riding bloomers had been worn before the war, but by 1917 *Vogue* was suggesting that women carry a discreet rucksack to put their skirts in at the moment of descent.

Sport had not yet acquired its health-giving image, and team spirit was not fostered in women. Perhaps for this reason riding was the sport of the decade since it combined practicality (riding was still a useful means of transport) with a sense of decorum and grace. Riding habits for those women who were bold enough to try riding astride were initially voluminous divided skirts, but breeches and paddock coats were soon approved. (Polo furthered the cause of the astride rider, since to play side saddle was impossible.) For these brave horsewomen, however, the penalty was to forego the elegant and imposing high silk hat; for them the low, broad, felt derby was sufficient, and for summer a black straw sailor hat. Because the early side-saddle habits were positively dangerous during a fall – tending to get caught up in the saddle – the apron or 'safety' skirt was developed, with a line of snap fasteners which ripped open in case of accident. It was just half a skirt which did not go under the rider at all, merely extending from the right knee (which rested over the pommel), to the left side; on the right it was only long enough to reach from the waist to the top of the saddle.

Habit fabrics varied, but flecked wool and heavy linen crash were particularly in demand. Colours, however, were no different from those of today. Grey or black were the most common, but the French asserted their originality by adopting blue or brown. The severity of these outfits was relieved by nosegays, black patent boots, white dogskin gauntlets, and of course the masculine element – pigskin puttees.

Tennis and golf were not forgotten in the rush to acquire skis and cars. 'What did the world do before golf became a pastime?' enquired *Vogue* in 1911, and articulated what has always characterized the sport: 'the costume for golf . . . always will be the same.' Lengths and fabrics have varied, but generally the emphasis has remained the same throughout this century: casual smartness. Tweed was used for most sports, but particularly for golf where even the essential tam-o'-shanter was tweed. (In summer, a tennis panama was worn.) Golf was the originator of the first 'casual' to filter into mainstream fashion: the sweater, first seen in 1919.

Accessories designed to complement tennis skirts and blouses were silk and wool cloaks to slip on after the game, canvas or buckskin espadrilles or even, mid-decade, lace-up tennis boots, high fashion with as many eyelets as possible, and black or white stockings; underneath, the ubiquitous corset.

By mid-war, sports houses had been set up to design attractive sportswear for the active woman. For the thousands of women who were driving ambulances, working in canteens and nursing the wounded behind the lines in France, these houses were invaluable since they had the active purpose in mind. The same house that could design a frivolous and startling cherry red sailor suit in woollen stockinette decorated with rayon pompons could also market a military overcoat for women and dungarees for the factory girl.

Generally, the more unusual the sport the more bizarre and ingenious the costume. Flying was even more thrilling than motoring, despite being reserved for the most privileged, and *Vogue* grudgingly acknowledged in 1917 that 'even in the field of aviation there are women with almost as much skill as the men'; and, with glee, that 'a special costume is a necessity.' It was certainly special: a short coat and wide breeches of leather, lined throughout with double-seamed blanket wool to exclude the icy air, and teamed with an aviator's crash helmet and high laced boots.

Women's preoccupation with masculinity led *Vogue* to plead in 1914 that 'if the waistcoat is cut, buttoned, pocketed, like a man's it may risk self-toned satin sleeves without compromising its sports reputation.' Dressing for sport was a battle to squeeze as much finery into the outfit as possible without it being obtrusive and, until function rather than frivolity or stifling propriety was revered, clothes remained so restrictive as to be worse than useless.

A motor bonnet with a 'becoming arrangement of mauve and purple veils.' AV 1911

This sports skirt features adjustable hem straps and buttons so that it can be raised at the wearer's discretion for the more demanding sports. AV 1911

For the 'new sport' of camping, nothing could be more efficient than the hooded 'slicker' for keeping out the damp. It is made of black, rubber-covered cambric sheeting. AV 1917

1920

BV 1919 Paul Iribe

The 'motor maid', *opposite*, draped in the longest and
smartest motoring coat, has adopted a huge Russian-style
toque, pompon trimmed. Even smarter is the motorist,
above, wearing a buckle-trimmed coat with matching gloves
and cap. The three buckled belts round the waist, echoed by
those at the wrist, protect her absolutely from icy draughts.
Her hands are kept freckle free by smart gloves. Ultimate
protection is provided by the personal windscreen, *right*,
supported by a shoulder frame and supplied with its own
yellow leather carrying case.

AV 1911   BV 1917

AV 1915

AV 1914

Spectators at the races, *above*, enjoying this sport reserved for men only. The spectator and the sportswoman meet, *left*. The long unbroken lines of the riding jacket contrast with the extravagance of the Poiret-influenced day wear outfit.

AV 1914

A different kind of spectator sport, *right:* the bun-bobbing contest with jelly-filled buns. The lucky girl to the left of the picture is young enough to be allowed to ride astride, wearing a version of the man's riding outfit.

This side-saddle habit, *above*, is not the 'safety' skirt type. It's bulkiness was both uncomfortable and dangerous. Behind the encumbered rider lies a more practical form of transport which was to overtake the horse in popularity.

AV 1918

Women enjoying their new sport of polo, *left and right*, wearing the strict uniform of white shirt, white stock, sleeveless khaki paddock coat, linen breeches, white helmet, lace-up boots and white chamois gloves.

AV 1913   AV 1913

AV 1914

A daring equestrian outfit, *left*, with the smartest lace-up boots and short coat which made inroads into the more sober, traditional style, *centre*. The smart children, *right*, wearing the predecessor of the hard hat, with unbraided hair, have been competing in a gymkhana. Fanny, on the left, 'has won again'.

AV 1917

AV 1918

AV 1915 Helen Dryden

These skaters, blissfully released from the hobble skirts introduced by Poiret in 1909, have adopted the most flared skirts they could find and have teamed them with the ever popular tam-o'-shanter and flamboyant stole. Poiret's oriental influence lingered, however, in this fantasy garment, *opposite*, with its lampshade silhouette and bloomers. Despite its patently imaginary nature, it does feature the much-used band of fur round its hemline, to weigh down the skirt for modesty's sake.

BV 1916 Steinmetz

AV 1914

AV 1914

BV 1919

Mr Waldorf Astor executing a difficult circle on the ice, *above*, while Princess Victoria Louise of Cumberland, the Kaiser's daughter, skates daintily round Kulm Lake, *above right*. The dashing man, *centre*, 'capped and trousered in the only convenient way', displays his tobogganing skills. For the most serious tobogganer, the Cresta Run, then as now, was the world's most notorious bob sleigh course; even in the eighties, it is still barred to women except for one day of every year. The couple dancing on the ice, *below left*, display the relative practicality of the man's skating outfit, versus the woman's attire. Chairs on runners, *below centre*, are an exhilarating means of crossing the ice for the novice. The girls, *below*, have taken full advantage of the vogue for fur on the ice, an ostentation forbidden the motorist, and are cosily protected against tumbles and frost-bite.

AV 1914

AV 1914

AV 1911

BV 1919 De Meyer

BV 1919 De Meyer

BV 1919 De Meyer

These early fashion shots at least make an attempt to suggest activity, although they have obviously been taken indoors against intricate backdrops. The snow-shoer, *left*, wears tweed breeches, a short camel hair coat and a hat of tan duvetyn. The smoke-grey velveteen skirt of the skater, *above*, is faced with a wide silk band which prevents it clinging awkwardly to the legs. For the tobogganer, *above left*, the woolly gauntlets and beaver cloth tam-o'-shanter are useful additions to the snow-shoer's outfit.

AV 1913

AV 1913

AV 1911

The inelegance and incompetence of the two girls, *above left and right*, are excused by the bulkiness of their clothes. The golfers, *centre*, wear huge hats and narrow ankle-length skirts, one of which is daringly front buttoned. For the cyclist, *below* *left*, the restrictive story is much the same: her tie, the one masculine detail she has borrowed, does not aid movement. The mixed baseball game, *below right*, must have been hopelessly contested by the women in this kind of outfit.

AV 1914   AV 1914

Mrs Irene Castle, a world-famous dancer of the time, poses balletically as a tennis player, *right*, in a white silk blouse laced with black ribbon and a double-belted skirt. More dressing-up games, *below*, with Mrs Castle as the huntress, golfer and horsewoman. The huntress's silhouette is unusually masculine, as she wears breeches without the normal skirt on top. As horsewoman, she wears white tricotine breeches and grey tweed jacket with the bottom button left unfastened in the smartest fashion.

AV 1917 De Meyer

AV 1917 De Meyer

AV 1917 De Meyer

AV 1917 De Meyer

1920

The astonishing aero wheel for the most dedicated fitness fanatic. FV 1929

A white velvet ensemble for skiing or skating; the skirt zips off to become a scarf. AV 1926 Redfern

'Sport has more to do than anything else with the evolution of the modern mode', said British *Vogue* in 1926; 'there is only one thing of which everyone is convinced . . . and that is the perfection of adaption to the needs of the game which modern dress has evolved.' Practicality in sportswear design was a new notion which became firmly established during the twenties. Leading this design field was Jean Patou, who accustomed the fashionable world to the idea of appearing 'undressed' in public during the day, removing sleeves from tennis dresses and designing a décolleté tennis dress incorporating a lapel which could be buttoned up to the neck after the game. Patou raised the hemlines of his sports dresses, and day-dress hemlines rose with them. By 1929 the suitability principle was so well established that when hemlines in general lengthened again, tennis dresses remained short.

From the mid twenties, the masculine silhouette in women's fashion became actively influential in freeing women from heavily layered sportswear, rather than being merely imitative. Suzanne Lenglen's boyish figure and cropped hair caught the imagination of the fashion conscious. The wide coloured bandeau she wore to match her sleeveless monogrammed cardigan swept across the tennis courts, meriting a *Punch* cartoon captioned: 'With the Lenglen bandeau tennis may at any moment develop into blind man's buff.' In 1927 Helen Wills, another major tennis star, adopted the subsequently much copied eye-shade. By the end of the decade it had become acceptable to play bare-headed. Although it had been usual since the beginning of the century to wear white for tennis, this was by no means universal. In 1920, *Vogue* recommended tennis hats in 'white cloth bound with black patent leather with black leaves and cherries' and, in 1924, a sky blue silk tennis dress striped with black and pleated to resemble a jumper suit.

In October 1921 the first knickerbocker golf suits appeared in American *Vogue*, and readers were commended on being 'more Amazon like'. For hunting, women and men wore similar garments on the upper torso but exposure of the leg's shape for women was a far slower development. For skating, skiing and fishing, women could wear men's breeches, provided that they wore a half-skirt too. In 1922 American *Vogue*, however, reprimanded those readers who chose to adopt men's equestrian style: 'Women cannot ride astride because most of them are not built that way. . . . If a woman insists upon riding like a man, please, oh, please let her consult a physician first . . . and then let me beg and implore her to ride and to dress like a gentleman, not like a chorus girl . . . for the pony ballet.'

Unlike mainstream fashion, sportswear made wide use of buttons and zips, to compromise between punctilious modesty and the active mood. In June 1920, for example, British *Vogue* showed a flying coat, the bottom half of which buttoned to form trousers during flight; gloves were attached to the sleeves with buckles. The bifurcated skirt was acceptable for skating, while in 1926 A. J. Suzanne Talbot designed a chambray tennis dress with a trouser skirt concealed by quantities of pleats.

One-piece garments were now considered more suitable than two-pieces for sport, but designers began to deviate. Helen Wills favoured a Patou skirt and shirt for tennis and in 1922 the House of James showed a white tricot skating costume trimmed with a wide hip-band of brushed wool, creating the impression of a two-piece.

Gabardine was a new fabric and it quickly superseded tweed, plaid and camel hair for winter sports since it was light, warm, snowproof and well ventilated. By the late twenties the peacock blues and poppy reds of the earlier years had faded into more sombre colours, and in particular to 'quicksilver' (shot grey and beige). Spotted baby calf-skin and black leather were used for skiing ensembles, and horse hide, chromed to make it waterproof yet pliable, was adopted for ski mittens. White was considered to compare unfavourably with the snow's brilliant whiteness and was forbidden for golf. For the latter, Chanel's favourite fabric, jersey, which had 'elasticity in action' and 'slender lines in repose', was used. In 1920 *Vogue* had asserted that, for tennis, 'a white knitted wool frock offers a cool front to the sun and a warm shoulder to the wind' but by the end of the decade such optimistic promises about versatility were discarded along with unsuitable materials like wool and jersey; lightweight washable silks and crepe de chine had taken their place.

It was not just new fabrics that were appearing during this time, but new sports for women too. The newest and most revolutionary activities were calisthenics, keep-fit exercises and squash. *Vogue* said in 1928 that 'a woman who can stand on her head in the bedroom is likely to have better poise in the drawing room.' Other ways of keeping fit included throwing the medicine ball (a huge beachball which had to be kept in motion without it hitting the ground), being massaged by a wide electric belt, working a rowing machine, or riding a mechanical horse – which, said *Vogue*, 'trots or canters without leaving its pedestal'. But most unusual was the giant aero wheel, propelled by transferring one's weight from one cross-bar to the next.

In rigidly traditional sports like riding, and for golf where specially designed sportswear was not essential, remnants of the old etiquette remained. The golfer was forbidden decorative pleats and allowed only sober inverted pleats at the side or front to facilitate movement. American *Vogue* said in 1925 that the woman with the wrong kind of sports clothes has 'probably lost her balance both mentally and otherwise and when she finally hits the ball she does it in a confused swirl of wrong motions, terminating in some awkward posture accentuated by her lack of smartness.' Despite the refreshing influences of Patou and Chanel, the metamorphosis had not yet been effected.

Suzanne Lenglen and Patou outfit. A V 1926 *Patou*

Helen Wills and visor. A V 1928 *Patou*

1930

BV 1920 Lepape

The dashing motorist, *left*, competes with the sun and her shining car for attention, and wins. The long, slender dress printed with dazzling zig-zags caters for the most extravagant tastes, while the smart long gloves and sleek, head-hugging cap add a note of professionalism. The imposing figure, *above*, wears a more practical outfit – a huge, military-style overcoat with a collar that fastens tightly up to the neck for rainproofing, and the same fashionable cap and gloves. The 'motor maid', *right*, combines utility and fashion in her ensemble. The button-on gilet and peaked fur cap are offset by embroidered gloves and the trailing scarf – like the one which strangled Isadora Duncan in 1927 when it caught in one of the wheels of her car.

FV 1924 Lepape

BV 1920 Lepape

These Schiaparelli flying outfits, *left*, in rubberized crepe, with their comfortable wide sleeves, are intended for the traveller rather than the aviator. The decorative buttons favoured by Schiaparelli serve no sporting purpose, but the cloches, derivative of the aviator's cap, protect the hair from the wind. The aviator gazing at the clouds, *opposite above left*, is wearing a mink-trimmed suede suit. The outfit, *opposite above right*, is of 'knitted chine woollen' with a gros-grain trim. The cosy helmet buckles onto the frock for wind-proofing. Viscountess de Siboure, *opposite below right*, sports an unusually masculine kit for absolute efficiency in the air, unlike the woman, *opposite below left*, perching precariously on the wing of her aircraft in high-heeled shoes.

F V 1928 Hoyningen-Huené. *Schiaparelli*

BV 1920

BV 1926

FV 1929

FV 1929

25

The first knickerbocker suit for women emerged in 1921, but men still had the strongest claim to it. The women looking on, *above*, are wearing the new jumpers. The relative suitability of the golfing outfits, *right and opposite*,

is highlighted by the inactivity of one and the expertise of the other. The woman, *left*, has adopted the pleats forbidden for golf, while the golfer, *opposite*, sports a sleek and exemplary outfit.

FV 1928 Steichen. *Williams and Cleaver*

FV 1928 Steichen. *Saks*

AV 1924 *Nardi*

The jaunty rider, *above left*, displays another radical development, apart from her astride riding preference: a contrasting jacket of heavy brown tweed and beige gabardine jodphurs. The side-saddle rider, *above right*, would not dream of such a contrast. Her habit is in immaculate dark blue melton cloth worn with a black bowler hat, a white silk stock, a canary yellow flannel waistcoat and a black bowler hat. For formal occasions, if the woman insists on riding astride, *below left*, matching breeches and jacket *must* be worn, with a stock and a derby hat.

AV 1920 Helen Dryden

AV 1924 *Nardi*

Astride riding, having seen an upsurge in interest during the war years, began to be ignored by the most fashionable. The side-saddle rider looking derisorily at her outdated companion, *above left*, is wearing a habit of natural pongee silk topped by a rough straw hat. The smart horsewoman, *right*, is sporting the popular 'safety' skirt, long at the front, short and draped at the back. Although the imposing couple, *below left*, have adopted opposing styles, the cut of both outfits is equally masculine. The felt derby has been adopted by the astride rider since it is more informal and in keeping with her attire. Note the diagonal cut of the breeches' knee seams which prevents the fabric from stretching.

BV 1927 Bolin. *Busvine*

Skiing twenties-style: the Lelong outfits, *opposite below left*, with their accentuated hiplines, are conspicuously earlier than the other three. These two tunics with breeches beneath are of heavy wool with fur trim – unlike the others which are waterproof. The stunning outfits, *left and opposite right*, made imposing *Vogue* covers, but the mood by this time was for sombre colours, such as those worn by the skiers in the background of the picture *opposite right*. Both these figures and the one *opposite above left* reveal the men's Norwegian-style trousers recently adopted by women.

BV 1927 Pierre Mourgu

BV 1928 Jean Pagès

w 1929 Eric. *Bessé*

w 1924 Lee Creelman Erickson. *Lelong*

VOGUE

BV 1928 Harriet Meserole. *Wanamaker (left and right), Bonwit Teller (centre)*

AV 1929 *Saks*

The hemline of the dress, *above*, is comparatively short, seen against the spectators' dresses, *opposite*. Even for men it was permissible to undress only so far, judging by the shocked look of these girls. Box pleats and intricate tucking on the sleeveless dresses, *above left*, create a stylish and efficient impression. The Patou eye-shade worn by the girl second from the left combines Suzanne Lenglen's bandeau with Helen Wills' eye-shade. The player to the right of this picture is wearing a crepe de chine U-backed dress which allows for an even tan, useful for evening décolletage, and anticipates the vogue for backless dresses in the thirties. The girl, *above*, is wearing a two-piece outfit, unusual at the time, although the two-piece of the kind featuring a matching flannel cape, *below left*, is not.

AV 1928 *Lord & Taylor*

FV 1925 L. Fellows

1930

Transparent oilskins and tortoiseshell-rimmed glasses are the height of fashion for the skier. FV 1936 *Schiaparelli*

Miss Sonja Henie, the eighteen-year-old world skating champion, enjoys a cooling drink at London's Grosvenor Road Ice Club. The allure of her black velvet, fur trimmed outfit – of which she had twenty-six identical examples – can't be beaten. BV 1930

Skiing, the sport of the decade, had become a thrilling religion. On the slopes a new professionalism appeared, bringing understatement in ski clothes; ski boots were the only obvious indication of the wearer's destination. *Vogue* advised its readers to guard against the 'unfettered fantasy' of the previous decade.

Between 1930 and 1933 the smart ski silhouette for men and women was long and narrow. Waists were accentuated by short, double-breasted, boxy jackets with the broad shoulders introduced by Schiaparelli, and wide lapels, worn with long Norwegian-style trousers with gathered hems (the precursors of plus-fours). Dark colours gradually gave way to vibrant hues, the transition effected by the addition of bright details in piping, facings and accessories. Schiaparelli and Patou designed two-tone suits, and designer Vera Borea interpreted the trend by wearing two-tone gloves at St Moritz in 1936. White, formerly frowned upon for skiing, now became, like the wearing of skirts on the slopes, associated with expertise: French *Vogue* noted how the British, still loyal to dark blue suits, added a sombre note. Far from sombre was the new mountain sunbathing craze. M. Rauch designed a low-backed swimsuit now that backs had taken over from legs as the focal point, and later versions had back panels which rolled down into pouches at the waist for maximum sun exposure. Patou even introduced a range of mountain sun-tan lotions.

Backs were in vogue on the tennis court, too: bows nestling in the small of the back, buttons and contrast trimmings gave emphasis to backless tennis dresses. The halter neckline was part of the same trend. Tennis cardigans lost popularity in favour of matching tennis ensembles including a coat, usually in silk or tweed. Volume for tennis skirts was now achieved by goring and bias cut, rather than pleats.

Much more shocking at the time were two events which were to have a lasting effect on tennis fashion: in 1931 Mrs Fearnley-Whittingstall appeared stockingless on court, and in 1933 Alice Marble wore shorts at Wimbledon. Two-piece shirt-and-shorts suits, popular in America, had permeated British fashion by 1936 and gradually evolved into the 'shorts dress' which buttoned up each side. In 1939, however, British *Vogue* said: 'there's a new rule in tennis; dress up for the game! The nude limbs that sprawled over the courts last year look utterly démodé. . . . short or even long sleeves cover arms, pleated dresses or trousers replace microscopic shorts.' Washable silk and linen were popular, as were the new crepe marocain and broadcloth.

Sportswear became both practical and chic, in keeping with women's changing attitudes. In the twenties there had been no need, for example, for the now fashionable pockets in shooting clothes, as men had been expected to carry the ammunition. British *Vogue* noted in 1935 that women 'meet men as equals . . . they carry their own packs, wax their own skis.' Schiaparelli concentrated on practicality, and by 1936 her transparent oilskins and white- or tortoiseshell-rimmed ski goggles were high fashion.

Waterproofed fabrics – gabardine, silk, wool, cord, jersey – were newly important in thirties ski wear. Lastex yarn, too, was a recent contributor to comfort and efficiency and was used by Vera Borea at the ankles of ski trousers as an alternative to waterproof gaiters. British *Vogue* announced in 1934 that 'no account of golf equipment is stop press news without the first details of the use of "lastex" yarn . . . which may well solve the problem of the "bulge" in front', and French *Vogue* declared that a 'jacket with a triangular lastex insertion in the back gives freedom of movement.'

The refreshing, bright colours for skiing were also evident on the golf course. Suede jackets in vivid lobster red, billiard green and bright blue dazzled sportswear fashion; double-breasted, with long revers and a belt, they had collars that could be fastened against the rain. Although by 1939 more women were appearing in slacks, golf wear remained comparatively formal, especially in Britain. Here, society golfers demanded smart outfits which could be worn all day in the country. In keeping with the formality which *Vogue* advised for golf was the golf bag with make-up compartment, so that running repairs could be made round the course.

The 'one- or two-piece' argument was still raging. Celebrated golfer Mollie Goyrlay told *Vogue* in 1934 that she disliked 'any form of one-piece garment; anything hung from the shoulders impedes balance.' In the same year Lillywhites compromised with a grey linen tweed outfit, its blouse and skirt held together by a pigskin belt slotted through metal links. Co-ordinating outfits, allowing adaptation to weather conditions, were popular, too: Burberry produced a wraparound skirt with matching tailored short jacket, one side of which was tweed and the other waterproof.

The most popular fabric for golf was still tweed, interest being added with contrast colours and accessories: matching gloves and gauntlets worn together, flamboyant decorative buttons and zips on the diagonal. The culottes which sporting addicts adopted to counter the movement towards longer skirts were worn for fishing, golf and shooting. Many shooting outfits were brightened by a Tyrolean touch: embroidered braces or Loden capes.

The thirties witnessed an increasing interest in active sport: punch-bag, water-skiing, running, fencing and mountaineering. For fencing the flared skirt first seen on the ice rink was worn. Riding was less popular, but attention was still given to the correct attire. The emphasis on tailoring for sports clothes was such that *Vogue* advised readers to take their saddle with them to fittings!

Fencing for women was new, practised in flared pleated skirts. B V 1937

Fascination for fitness and poise led to the adoption of yoga. This exponent demonstrates the 'tree' position. F V 1938

1940

The battle is on: shorts versus dresses, short socks versus long ones, short skirts versus long skirts. The choice of sports clothes was no longer a matter of propriety but of fashion and preference. All the dresses here have gored rather than pleated skirts; what pleats there are appear on divided skirts. Shoulders are becoming wider, and the waistline has resumed its natural position – the girl playing tennis, *opposite above*, is wearing a dress whose back plunges to this new waistline. Suzanne Lenglen's cardigan and bandeau have been discarded in favour of coats and eye-shades or bare heads. Sport has asserted itself as an integral part of the decade's social life.

BV 1934

BV 1935 Libis

v 1932 Jean Pagès

This graceful player, *left*, anticipates *Vogue*'s advice to 'dress up for the game.' The length of her skirt and sleeves characterizes the smartest thirties look. The sailor, *right*, lounging casually in the latest beach trousers, undermines her exemplary sporting outfit by the bangles adopted from Nancy Cunard, *Vogue*'s Paris correspondant.

BV 1931 Jean Pagès

with VOGU
PATTE

SUMMER FASHION

FV 1936 Schall. *Rochas*

FV 1936 Schall. *Bessé (left),
Schiaparelli (centre), Heim (right)*

Bicycles have summarily dismissed
the car and the horse as the most
thrilling form of transport. The
exhausted biker, *opposite*, and the
girls, *above and near right*, are perfect
examples of the best-dressed fitness
addict. Dungarees or shorts made of
flannel, leather and tweed teamed
with masculine shirts, socks and
lace-up shoes, are more suitable
than the precarious panama and
tight skirt of the tandem rider,
far right.

FV 1936 Schall

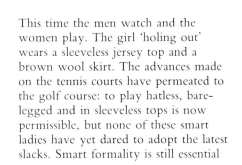

This time the men watch and the women play. The girl 'holing out' wears a sleeveless jersey top and a brown wool skirt. The advances made on the tennis courts have permeated to the golf course: to play hatless, bare-legged and in sleeveless tops is now permissible, but none of these smart ladies have yet dared to adopt the latest slacks. Smart formality is still essential for the golfer – hence the well-cut suits, silver buttons and foulard scarves these women are wearing.

AV 1932 Libis. *Women's clothes, left to right: O'Rossen, Madeleine de Rauch, Lucile Paray, Chantal, Lucile Paray, Madeleine de Rauch, Martial et Armand, Redfern, Philippe et Gaston, Mirande, Philippe et Gaston*

FV 1935 Schall. *Busvine*

FV 1935 Schall. *Knizé*

FV 1939 E. Lindner. *Lomaz (top) R. R.*
Bunting (shoe), Hermès (belt)

Stark, masculine chic characterizes these outfits. Variations on trousers are essential for shooting – divided skirts, shorts, plus-fours and jodhpurs. The striking game shot, *opposite right*, has been influenced by the Tyrolean trend first spotted on the golf course, noticeable in the smart trim down the side of her linen shorts and the breast pockets of the tailored jacket, in the long socks and the jaunty felt hat. The couple, *opposite left*, are more traditional with their tweed plus-four suit and jodhpurs and jumper. The masculine element is still prevalent in the cravat and sturdy shoes shown in the drawing, *opposite below*. The tweed suit, *right*, combines femininity in the pretty bow and chunky studded boots.

FV 1939 Agneta Fischer

The thrilling exertions of the skier contributed to the development of less restrictive sportswear. Women ignored the constraints imposed on the golfer or horsewoman and adopted the most convenient clothes. Women had been taking part in the Olympics since 1928, and their participation in competitive ski events was now common, *below left*. The most professional skiers slipped on the latest goggles for absolute efficiency. Lastex bands round the ankles, *left*, aid water-tightness. The sleekest Norwegian-style trousers, tucked into the boots, are cosily matched with an unusual sheepskin coat, *below*.

FV 1936 Schall. *Jacques Heim*

FV 1936 Schall. *Madeleine de Rauch*

FV 1938 Schall

BV 1936

1940

This W.A.A.F. Balloon Operator is equipped with oilskins for bad weather. All-women crews took charge of many balloon sites. BV 1943.

Propaganda prints were a mid-war craze. This poster-strewn playsuit is designed with an eye to export. BV 1942.

Fabric restrictions, introduced in 1941 in Britain and in 1942 in America, had a drastic effect on the production of sportswear which was, naturally, of minor importance. Availability and styles were limited; dresses could not have more than five buttons, seaming was minimal and yardage around the hem was restricted. By the end of the war it had become impossible to buy a tennis dress. One advantage brought by rationing, however, was the adoption of slacks for sport and the women's services, due to the shortage of stockings.

In the early forties a peak of utilitarianism was reached. For the next thirty years sportswear, rather than leading general fashion development as it had done since the twenties, was to develop independently. It merely echoed street fashion, following the stark, feminist mood of the early forties, later veering towards femininity when Dior's 'New Look' of 1947 catapulted into fashion.

In 1941 American *Vogue* described a 'growing intolerance for anything but classic simplicity in ski clothes'. A symptom of this intolerance was the new slimmed-down ski trousers: proofed gabardine trousers eventually became as clinging as tights. Because of the inelasticity of the fabric, however, thigh-to-knee zips were added. These were undone for ease of movement in action and zipped up for *après-ski*, giving a sleek line. The severity of this look was compounded by the vogue for black ski wear, sometimes relieved by decorative Norwegian sweaters or flashes of magenta. Gaiters had disappeared except for occasional use with the gauchos which Hermès tried unsuccessfully to introduce. The experts once again distinguished themselves by wearing short, divided, box-pleated skirts and bibs, with polo-necked jumpers.

Anorak styles changed little, except that the parka, elongated and tight-waisted, became as popular as the waist-length jacket. Russian ponyskin was popular for jackets, being supple, elegant and ideal for *après-ski* when teamed with cashmere sleeves and ocelot *après-ski* boots. Beneath this garb, *Vogue* suggested, bulky long-johns should be discarded in favour of one-piece 'maillots' with long legs. Amusing, too, was the string vest providing a layer of warm air between the body and the overgarments. For less cold weather *Vogue* showed skiers in trousers and bandeau tops for the first time in 1942.

The demand for well-fitting ski boots led to complicated systems of double lacing and intricate back lacing from the heel to the top of the boot. Ski goggles were changing too, to accommodate interchangeable lenses: yellow for dull days and black for bright sunlight.

The austere silhouette was so popular that the fluffy outline of the hair was considered undesirable; a square of gabardine was designed to conceal it, with a central hole through which the face could be slipped, and ends to be tied at the back of the neck. Salopettes were new, influenced by the now familiar garb of the factory worker and the land girl. They were generally sleeveless, but some long-sleeved and front-zipped models appeared on the market. One particularly smart variation featured in *Vogue* was grey gabardine with a diagonal-fastening jacket, zipped to the back of the trousers for a smooth fit, anticipating styles of the seventies and eighties.

In the early forties goring was still modish for tennis – sometimes as many as ten panels were used – but by the end of the decade pleats were fashionable again for dresses teamed with their own knickers. In 1949 Gussi Moran appeared at Wimbledon in her notorious lace-trimmed knickers designed by Teddy Tinling. Tinling was accused of putting 'sin and vulgarity into tennis', but soon lace was to be seen on ski wear, swimwear and play clothes. Badminton players had more freedom in their choice of clothes, and could wear halter-neck bikini tops and slim-waisted skirts.

Tennis wear was normally made from practical rayon jersey or rayon sharkskin, featuring cap sleeves and padded shoulders. This apotheosis of synthetics was endorsed by Tinling's apposite question: 'Why should we wear the same materials as Jesus Christ?'

Cycling was very popular, and short skirts which just covered the back of the saddle were highly suitable. Alternatively, American-influenced play clothes such as pinafore dresses with black wool tights or socks were worn – for bowls, darts and motorbiking, too. Winter cyclists adopted the gaiters now abandoned by skiers. Schiaparelli's innovative style continued to startle the fashion world and she marketed some dark fur culottes for cycling. Skating clothes had changed little since the thirties: skirts were still circular, but slightly longer and the fur hemline trim had become taffeta.

Points of interest for country sports were long socks, lace-up shoes and buckskin pouches swinging from belts. Neat hairstyles were as in demand as they were for skiing, and *Vogue* advised the wearing of brown leather open-topped overstitched helmets to keep the hair tidy. Golf clothes did not change except that padded shoulders became more emphatic, hips narrower and waists more defined. Collarless shirts were the most distinctive new addition. For riding, jodphurs with pronounced 'wings' at the sides and long narrow legs were worn with tweed jackets.

In 1948 American *Vogue* took an unprecedented step, forbidding the observation of fashion trends for shooting attire. 'Forget your waistline; you're there to shoot. Except for shooting driven bird, never wear a skirt, you need pants for protection against brush and cold. . . . As invisibility is their main objective, shooting clothes . . . should blend in with the terrain; khakis, tans, field greens.' Sportswear, now and for the next ten years, was driving itself into a design cul-de-sac, a result both of wartime stringencies and, ironically, because of the striving for practicality which had characterized the twenties and thirties.

A gabardine square which ties round the back of the neck for the cleanest skiing silhouette. FV 1947 Nepo. *Madeleine de Rauch*

The navy swing blazer for tennis. AV 1941. *D. Ritter, Ltd*

A knitted ski top made backless for tanning by a strip which rolls down into a military-style waist pack. BV 1946 *Schiaparelli*

1950

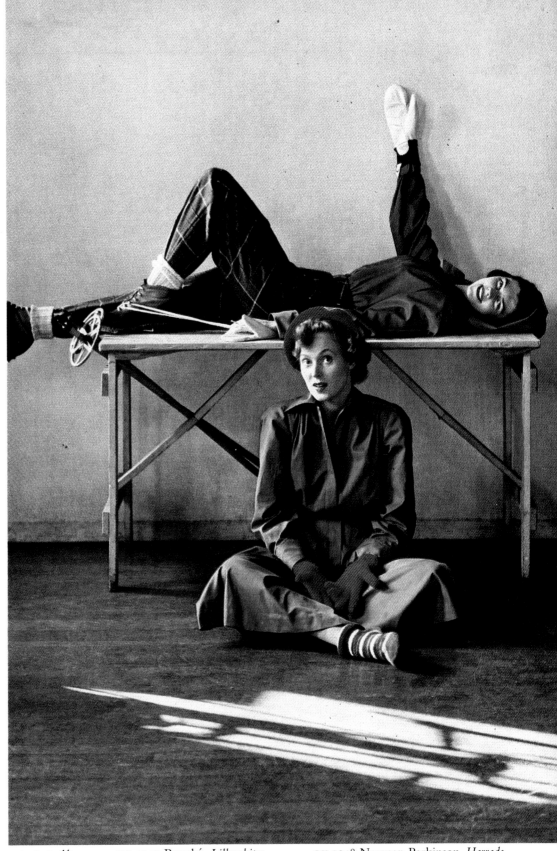

Stream-lining was by now so revered that any excess fabric was forbidden. Ski trousers had slimmed down, *opposite*, so that they were now more like tights. The dungarees of the munitions worker influenced the cut of the matching jerkin, which gives the effect of an all-in-one suit. The gabardine skirt, *top*, is for the expert only. The more amateur skier, *above*, contents herself with a balaclava. The proofed cotton gabardine skirt-suit, *right*, can be teamed with plaid trousers.

AV 1940 Toni Frissell. *Vera Maxwell*

AV 1941 *Altman*   BV 1949 Bouché. *Lillywhites*   BV 1948 Norman Parkinson. *Harrods*

Shorts, shirts and
socks were now
sufficient for
almost any sport.
The oarswoman
sports a sombre
version, *opposite*,
and then, *right*,
adds a bright scarf
to her box-pleated
divided skirt. Both
outfits are made of
the synthetics so
invaluable to the
forties sports-
woman for their
hard-wearing and
quick-drying
qualities.

AV 1943 Toni
Frissell.
*Abercrombie &
Fitch*

AV 1944 Penn. *Claire McCardell*

Centre: AV 1940 Horst. *Lord & Taylor*

During the war years, America took the lead in sportswear development once again. The play clothes sent over by Claire McCardell were eagerly snatched up by the British. They could be worn for bowling, badminton, cycling, or just walking the dog. *Opposite, left to right, top to bottom:* black wool jersey slacks and jacket; knitted wool pinafore, polka-dot shirt and pants; little-boy tartan pants and lumberjack top; doll dress of red-striped wool jersey over skin-fitting red wool jersey underpants; fringed wool tartan shorts; wool wrapped skirt and jersey top, over red pants. Exercise was such an integral part of women's lives by now that *Vogue* designed a cover, *opposite centre,* incorporating keep-fit addicts. Another obsession, in America as in Britain, was 'women in defense', *right.*

VOGUE

WOMEN IN DEFENSE
America Trains for 18 Skills

LONDON PORTFOLIO
Lady Reading's Message
R.A.F. Flyers

MID-SUMMER FASHIONS
for "More Taste Than Money"

JULY 1, 1941
PRICE 35 CENTS
40 CENTS IN CANADA

see section facing page

AV 1944 Penn. *Claire McCardell* (centre: *Duchess Royal*)

AV 1941 Toni Frissell

As a result of wartime sufferings and stringencies, the note struck by *Vogue* was one of forced optimism, saying of the girl, *right*, 'She's high on a hill: where she's got by her own effort. No road map of the future bewilders her.' In days of petrol rationing, cycling was cheap, fun and beneficial. Claire McCardell's wool jersey hooded top, tweed breeches and waist pouch, *opposite left*, are sleek and warm for winter cycling. The cyclists, *opposite centre*, wear cheap navy and white regatta cloth; the demure woman, *opposite above*, wears a divided skirt and tailored jacket which can be used for ordinary day-time wear too. The shorts, *opposite below*, of silk shantung can be topped with a gingham skirt for colder days.

1950

The polo collar, *top*, forms a hood while the cap, *above*, is knotted wittily behind. BV 1952 Francis McLaughlin. *Rima* (*top*). BV 1954 Hammarskiöld. *Jaeger*

Prints are essential. This turquoise and white printed ski anorak has an all-in-one hood which draws close round the face for blizzard conditions. BV 1957 Silverstein. *Kriesemer*

The harshness of the forties lingered on in the early fifties, but gradually the by now stale designs of the post-war period were transformed into the startling styles of the sixties. As in the twenties, that other period of transition when previously unknown heights of practicality were achieved by adding drapes and sashes to conceal what might have been called improper clothes, the impulse of fifties sportswear was to add accessories, flamboyant collars and fake fur to the old style. At last teenagers rejected the craving to imitate their mothers' styles of dress.

The straight sleeves featured on anoraks in the forties were gradually eased into a fuller, batwing shape, initially by the introduction of wide strips of lastex running along the inside of the arm to the wrist. This new volume manifested itself in the body of anoraks, too: artists' smocks, belted or otherwise, and balloon-shaped jackets were popular. Colour was reinstated, and *Vogue* once again advocated 'a note of fantasy' in ski attire. Vivid shades of pink, the latest colour, could be achieved by more sophisticated dyeing processes. In 1955 *Vogue* featured a pink blouson lined with white in waterproof poplin, smocked on the hips. Quilting was common now and stylish when executed on red taffeta. Collars in contrasting colours became so large that they often turned into balaclavas or hoods. Ingenuity in hood design led to zipped collars into which the hood could be slipped when not in use.

Amidst these exciting developments functionalism was not forgotten. Gloves with zippered pockets on top of the palms made it easy to find your ski pass, and pockets across the front of jackets made convenient sandwich carriers. Spring ski wear combined the vogue for layers with coolness by the use of fake jumpers – merely bibs with polo necks worn under turtle-neck sweaters. Fake fur united warmth with durability: fake zebra was striking and in line with the trend for gaily or geometric patterned anoraks. Elasticated cloth eliminated the need for side zips in ski trousers, and straps under the feet gave a new tautness; by 1956, striped trousers were high fashion. In the 1953 Olympics the Austrian skiing team appeared in 'two-in-one boots' – the inside boot was made of suede and could be worn by itself for *après-ski*, but improved contact with the outer boot for skiing.

The demand for a strict, rigid uniform for sportswear was fading by the mid fifties, and what became known as the 'sporty' look prevailed. Golf was rewarded at last by really informal clothes: bermudas from California began to permeate Britain, although culottes were still popular too. Flannel or corduroy slacks had become permissible, even at tournament level, worn with turtle-neck sweaters and smart tartan scarves. In 1959 Hermès made a turtle-neck sweater in three different colours – one each for the sleeves and a third for the body – but for the more traditional golfer white sharkskin dresses with cap sleeves were highly acceptable, particularly when the sleeves were slit to the shoulder to facilitate energetic drives. The most fashionable kind of jacket was made of soft leather in pale, clear colours.

In 1954 permanent pleating appeared on the sportswear scene, and knife-pleated skirts became essential tennis wear since they were smart and easy to look after. The puckered nylon introduced in 1949 dried in fifteen minutes and quickly became very well established for all sports. Tennis shorts had become exceptionally short by 1951, and were sometimes ingeniously trimmed with stripes down each leg to conceal zip fasteners. Generally, however, tennis wear, influenced by Dior's 'New Look' of 1947, was becoming more feminine – a typical outfit was Teddy Tinling's white waffle piqué dress with a high scalloped neckline and scalloped skirt flared at hip level. His, too, was the idea of designing clothes to characterize his clients. In 1953, for example, he designed a dress for Maureen Connolly trimmed with crowns, anticipating her meteoric rise to fame. He later designed a dress for Virginia Wade with a shark's teeth hemline which he felt 'expressed her predatory personality'. Chanel was not to be left out of the couture tennis wear field and she produced a thick white wool jersey trench coat for going to and from the court.

There was a new need for casual clothes for a more sporting lifestyle, particularly for motorbikes and Vespas. For these, a fake leopardskin top with a cowl neck, jersey slacks and suede chukka boots were eminently suitable. Cycling remained as popular as ever and trousers for this sport followed the pattern of ski pants, narrowing considerably.

Sailing clothes were ruled by the same practical requirements as those for shooting had been in the forties. In 1959 *Vogue* asserted that 'looks are of secondary importance as long as *you* are warm and dry, and can afford to get wet and dirty without giving it a moment's thought.' Proofed nylon anoraks were less bulky than oilskins and, despite *Vogue*'s warnings to ignore fashion, there were numerous models on the market which followed the trend for gaily patterned skiing anoraks. In 1958 *Vogue* featured a white Taco cotton jacket printed with a school of fantastic fish, orange-piped to match the trousers. Trousers were generally made of blue denim and often side slit so that they could be rolled up easily. Informality and the absence of a fashionable impulse characterized shooting and fishing clothes, too. For fishing, waterproof overskirts and knee-buttoning whipcord leggings were still useful, in natural colours such as 'feuille morte'. Gaiters retained popularity, worn over narrow trousers for shooting.

Riding habits have neither influenced nor been influenced by fashion. Side-saddle riding was still common in the fifties, and generally the uniform remained the same. Rigidity of dress for riding has always distinguished the sport as a select club with its own unchangeable rules. By the start of the sixties formality was obsolete and horse riding went into decline.

The vogue for prettier, more decorative tennis dresses manifests itself in this thick white waffle piqué dress with a high, scalloped neckline and a skirt flaring from hip-level. BV 1956 Hammarskiöld. *Teddy Tinling*

A leopard-patterned pullover with elasticated hips, slacks and suede bootees doubles up for *après-ski* and Vespa riding. BV 1958 Vernier. *Leveson-Furrier*

1960

BV 1955 Henry Clarke. *Corvette*

AV 1955 Henry Clarke. *Masket Bros of Hope Skillman Cottons*

AV 1955

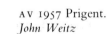
AV 1957 Prigent. *John Weitz*

Stripes and dots were at last enlivening sportswear; the 'sporty' look has expanded to include the new 'sloppy joe' and romper suit. The red and white towelling sweater, *opposite*, is flagrantly eye-catching and is teamed with a fringed stole tied piratically round the head. The same square-cut sleeves feature on the teeshirt *above left*. The water-skier, *below left*, wears a useful striped cover-up with sailor collar and open neck, teamed with rather less practical black suede shorts. The playsuit, *left*, is most flamboyant of all – white dotted piqué, back buttoned, self sashed, with the best of the fifties sunglasses.

Mondrian-style beach wear, which
combines startling shapes with the current
vogue for bright colours, especially pink.
The white 'sloppy joe' and blue jeans of
the mariner, *opposite*, are for the slightly
more serious sportswoman.

AV 1953 Penn

FV 1956 Bourdin. *Emilio*

Shorts, having opened up the tennis court as an arena for fashion as well as sport, have now been overtaken by the tennis dress again in the latest flush of femininity instigated by Dior. *From left to right*, short all-in-one linen play suit; the latest sailor-style poplin blouse and skirt with elasticated waist; sharkskin dress with roll collar, diagonal buttons, cap sleeves and flared skirt; romper suit with elasticated waist and legs; dress with a trapeze neckline which leaves the neck free, a slit skirt lending ease of movement and showing off decorative knickers beneath; linen dress with extravagantly pleated skirt.

Decorative details are essential for tennis now and relieve the stark lines of the knitted sharkskin shirt and shorts, *opposite*: the shorts have green piping and a back zip. The outfit is, unusually, completed by the addition of a cloche-brimmed cap on a hairnet.

FV 1951 *André Tunmer*
FV 1951 Arik Népo. *Vincent Mehnert*

BV 1954 Vernier. *Gordon Lowe*
FV 1952 *Galeries Lafayette*

BV 1950 Honeyman. *Gordon Lowe*
FV 1952 Jacques Boucher. *Palu Sports*

BV 1952 Norman Parkinson. *Jantzen*

BV 1955 Norman Parkinson. *Spectator Sports (left), Bogner (right)*

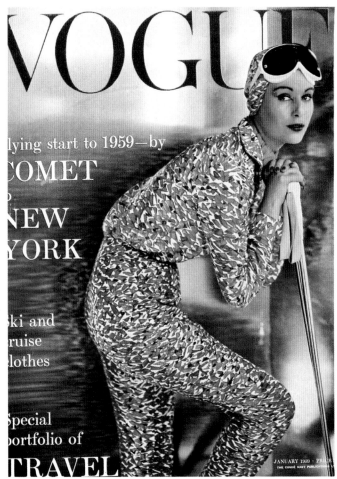

BV 1959 Vernier. *Emilio Pucci*

A huge volume of colour was building up on the slopes, eventually erupting into the blues, oranges and pinks for which the decade is remembered. *Below left,* slim-fitting vorlager trousers and battle jacket, with an amusing duck-billed cap, partnered with a four-piece ensemble of vorlager trousers, zippered jacket, hood and skirt (not shown). The girls, *above left,* display a sleeker and more colourful variation on the same idea. This time the trousers achieve their tautness by straps under the feet. The skier in blue wears a fleece-lined proofed poplin jacket, while her companion sports the latest elasticated spun nylon. The black and caramel checks, *opposite,* match the elasticized wool caramel trousers; the black ribbing of the cuffs is repeated on the peaked cap. This avalanche of colour was at its most intense by 1959 – as in the dazzling suit by Emilio Pucci, *above.* The shirt, trousers and hat are printed in an abstract brilliant turquoise, sap green and cherry design, offset by the brightest of red lipsticks. The days of playing sport without a hint of make-up were over.

BV 1950 Honeyman. *Fortnum & Mason (left), Lillywhites (right).*

BV 1958 Vernier. *Luis Ebste*

AV 1955 Prigent. *Smartee*

AV 1955 Prigent. *Jane Colby/Canterbury*

BV 1959 Norma
Parkinson. *Harr
Hall, Herbert
Johnson, How
Sportswear*

AV 1955 Prigent. *Bill Atkinson*

Vespas and motorbikes were the essential fashion accessories for the fifties girl. The biker, *opposite above left*, wears a sleeveless over-blouse of red cotton knit plaid, trimmed with black and worn with a pair of slim black pants and a white Orlon pullover. *Opposite above right*, a self-hooded Lambretta shirt with its unhooded, long sleeved sister. *Opposite below left*, a blanket-wool plaid cardigan in yellow, russet and brown with natural-coloured suede sleeves, matched with russet worsted flannel shorts and a smart beret. *Opposite below right*, smart slacks with a collared wool cardigan, suede shoes and the essential head-hugging cap. The hood, *right*, becomes a cowl neckline on warmer days. The hand-loomed white wool pullover tops a pair of red Milliken wool plaid knicker-bockers.

A V 1955 Prigent. *Columbia, Geist & Geist*

1960

This white mink tennis dress is also 'great form for the games people play at home', said *Vogue*. Here it is worn with striped, crushed silk tights. A V 1966 Horst. *Gunther Jaeckel Furs*

Black-studded white leather driving shoes. B V 1965 David Bailey. *Rayne*

In the sixties people began to play at being sporty. Yves Saint Laurent, Pierre Cardin and Courrèges led the field in fashion's new sporting look and produced dashing space-age clothes. These clothes were never designed or even worn for sport but the vital thing was that they *looked* as though they were. Such sportswear as *Vogue* featured took suitability to its extreme, like the Rayne white leather driving shoes studded with fantastical, asymmetric black rubber knobs. In 1966 the ultimate in excess appeared: a white mink tennis dress with striped, crushed silk tights. It was a vain decade where hair transplants and face lifts were the latest craze and sport for fitness went out of fashion.

The sixties tracksuit or 'thrill suit' was a much vaunted style of dress for sport and play. At its most impractical it was made of silver vinyl, the decade's favourite fabric and colour. Excitement over the first landing on the moon in 1969 boosted the vogue for tight boiler-suits like the blackberry-red leather one lined in silk featured by *Vogue*. Most startling of all was the 1965 fishnet playsuit with vinyl pockets concealing the breasts and hips. By 1970 this tawdry lushness, and the 'baby-doll' look, were beginning to pall, and healthy living was soon to become of prime importance.

Two major advances affected skiers in the sixties: the introduction of dry ski slopes and the development of clipped ski boots which quickly superseded the old laced type. In 1967 *Vogue* even displayed a black ski jacket which fastened wittily with the same clips. Renewed dedication to the sport led to further attempts to improve the efficiency of boots, and in 1969 a boot appeared moulded entirely from one piece of white plastic, lined with sheepskin.

The fur sweater, favoured by Audrey Hepburn, was eulogized by the fashionable in the sixties. Its most popular form was the drip-dry fake version. If the fur had to be real, then the more startling the better: blue fox for parkas, natural lynx belly vests and, most spectacular of all, purple fleecy lamb's-fur spats. A panoply of fake fur fabrics imitated all these, but made no attempt to assert their verisimilitude. American *Vogue* suggested adding to such contrivance by wearing really heavy make-up: 'the more glop you have on your face the better.'

Anoraks were breaking out in stripes, dots, daisies and checks; when these were insufficiently dazzling, new Jacquard weaves were included and sometimes intricate vertical lurex quilting, too. Sizzling orange and swipes of purple, yellow and silver dominated, but black and white were still a smart combination, particularly when featured on reversible anoraks with a sandwich of foam in between; Yves Saint Laurent used both colours on a suede skiing hood with a peaked cap and attached jersey cowl neck. Individualism was demanded but, for the experts, not at the expense of speed: lightness and wind resistance had become a prerequisite for ski suits. A mixture of silk and Helanca nylon produced a glossy surface designed to slice through the wind. Chunky plastic zips assisted in the quest for lightness.

As trouser flares swelled larger and larger for day wear, ski fashions retained their reputation for being the smartest of all sportswear, initially by a small slit at the bottom of the trousers which enabled them to splay over the boot, and then inner legs to tuck inside the boot with false bell-bottoms over the top. The advent of the miniskirt in 1965 ensured a more prominent place for the short skirt on the slopes – such as the mauve miniskirt with matching battle jacket, pink polo-neck sweater and perspex visored helmet or mirrored sunglasses. Hot pants featured strongly, too, as they answered the sixties preoccupation with accentuating the body.

In 1963 an important advance in warm, waterproof clothes for sport was made: the appearance of the Husky, a thermo-insulated jacket comprising a nylon shell and polyester filling. Since then, innumerable variations on this idea have been marketed for any sport played in damp, cold conditions.

Despite blistering changes in fashion outlook, certain sports retained some of their sedate and traditional image. 'Play golf and croquet in long skirts, tennis, fencing and cycling in brief bermudas', asserted *Vogue* in 1968. Some elements of the new look did permeate golf, however, such as the shiny, black vinyl knee-length skirt or madras shorts with knee-high socks and geometrically printed boat-neck tops, and the new battle jacket.

The transition between the old and the new was remarkably painless for tennis players, since the shape of the clothes adopted by the most stylish for day wear fitted the requirements for tennis exactly: very short, straight shifts and wide hairbands. For the first time since the twenties, coloured tennis dresses were permitted and, following the bare body trend, *Vogue* approved halter necks and cut-out midriffs.

Silicone-treated guernsey jumpers and navy stretch denim trousers with foot straps were acceptable for sailing. More striking was a white vinyl windbreak that zipped up to the chin to meet a baby cap of white patent leather at the top and tiny terry cloth shorts below. For colder days, hipster trousers with side laces from hip to ankle were advised, and for wet weather an electric blue hooded anorak with transparent wrists and ear patches which provided little windows when the head was turned. Grès' fishing kit was less practical: a shiny cinnamon-coloured belted leather tunic with crinkly leather muskrat-lined wading boots.

In 1969 *Vogue* remarked that 'Sportsclothes showed fashion how to be fast and free. Now they show how to steal the thunder from all the other competitors, with racing colours, great goggle glasses, hair binders, all-in-ones, second skin shapes, striding shorts.' Sportswear had come through a dark age once again and was about to become the greatest single influence on fashion up to the present moment.

For the individualist, Mrs Vernon J. Taylor's kit is exemplary. The two sporrans are invaluable for ski passes, and the amusing picture is completed by a soldier's cap from the American Civil War. AV 1969 Toni Frissell

The mini ascends the slopes. Here it is made of yellow nylon matelassé with a matching cap which tucks into the stand-up collar. AV 1966 William Klein. *Michele Rosier/White Stag*

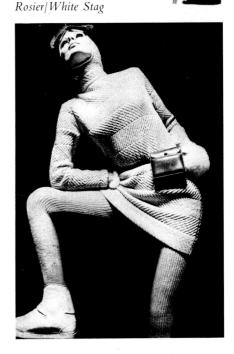

1970

BV 1966 Helmut Newton. *Kir, James Wedge, John Bates/Jean Varon*

Vinyl accelerates into top gear. *Above,* the cyclist wears slick black leather gloves, bare to the knuckles, a black, shirred and stretchy close-fitting helmet made in Celon Quiltastic with an orange perspex visor. Her tiny, brilliant matching dress with orange perspex hem by John Bates at Jean Varon accentuates her every movement. The biker, *right,* flaunts her shiny space boots in transparent vinyl, striped and capped in patent leather, and her domed leather helmet with its scorching orange perspex brim. The flagrantly showy jumpsuit which unites the two is of Celon jersey and ciré with a broad black leather hipster belt.

BV 1966 Helmut Newton. *Walter Steiger, James Wedge, John Bates/Jean Varon*

v 1966 Duffy.
Victoire

The sixties body-revealing obsession prevented sportswear from being really practical, as is displayed by this sailing suit, *left*. It is made entirely of plastic and vinyl, which might seem practical enough, but not when so much of the physique is on show through its transparent windows. Similarly, the motorist, *opposite*, with the latest Thunderbird offering a back seat which 'curves around like a love seat', is dressed to kill rather than to play sport. She wears a leotard of silvery white stretch fabric with a wide chained turtleneck, a space-queen helmet, white boots and pigskin gloves.

A V 1963 Gene Laurents. *Ulla*

The glaring plastic eye-balls, *opposite*, provide an interesting alternative to sober ski goggles. The equally startling skier, *right*, has taken every opportunity to flaunt the latest craze for fur. She wears a waterproof dandelion yellow fake fur jacket which buckles at the waist. The laced spats of Mongolian sheepskin represent the real fur element, but most striking of all are the new clipped ski boots.

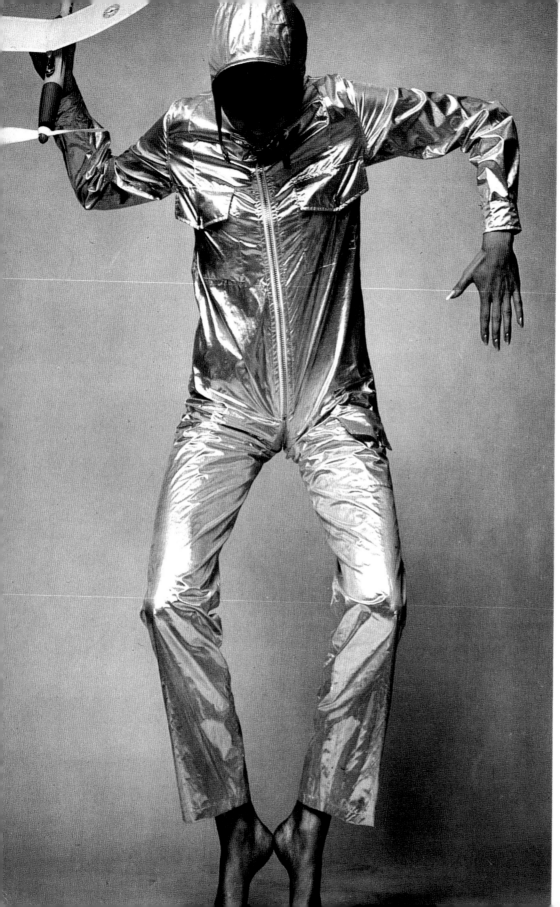

FV 1966 Guy Bourdin. *V de V, chez Tunmer*

BV 1967 Helmut Newton. *Aquascutum, Simone Mirman*

A variation on the aviator's suit, *left*, provides this nylon and lurex 'thrill suit', exemplary in its stylishness but not in its application to sport. Typically, the point accentuated by *Vogue* at this time was the new and exciting fake tan which had been applied to the model's hands and feet. Two further adaptations of the aviator's style appear *above and opposite*. Both are caricatures of what the flyer might wear, but what, on the whole, she did not. For the sixties woman, sport was once again a dressing-up game, just as it had been in the first years of this century; but this time sport gave credibility to the fantastical clothes that women were wearing, rather than enabling them to wear revealing clothes.

BV 1967 Helmut Newton. *Susan Sma*

1970

Flashy lycra, winged helmet. BV 1979
Albert Watson. *Gamba, Alpine Sports*

Outfit derived from the boxing ring.
BV 1978 Albert Watson. *Issey Miyake*

The hedonism of the sixties prevailed in the early seventies,. but was beginning to fade. People now had less money to spend, and even the synthetics now used so extensively were becoming increasingly expensive because of the leap in oil prices. A reaction against the tinselly lushness of the previous decade took the form of a fitness craze which has endured to the present day. Jog-ins took the place of love-ins, and new clothes which left the wearer prepared for action at all times surged onto the market. Fake tanning creams stole the limelight from false eyelashes on the make-up counters, and the demise of the platform sole was hastened by the influx of plimsolls of every colour and style.

With this new enthusiasm for sport, sportswear at last had a direct influence on day wear again; stretch velours and towelling tracksuits were even acceptable party wear provided that the colours were bright enough. In 1978 *Vogue* sported the first grey flecked cotton jersey, a fabric that was to dominate the market for four years.

In 1978 roller skating and roller disco sizzled onto the scene, following on from the mid-seventies skateboarding craze; for all three sports the new glossy, clinging lycra was found to be eminently suitable. Swanky Modes designed a lycra minidress, with bold cut-out shapes down each side, specifically for the disco. Leotards with short frilled skirts, cap sleeves, spots, stripes and rhinestones, worn with leg warmers, were suitable for dance, keep fit and even ice skating. In the late seventies, long loose tee shirts knotted at the hips were invaluable for roller skating. In 1980, Olympics year, *Vogue* readers glimpsed a cycling outfit from Condor Cycles which was so exemplary in its practicality that it was sported as fashion: long, skin-tight trousers with a striped jersey zipped at the neck, worn with soft kid lace-up jazz shoes. Bodybuilding and weightlifting for women were the crazes of 1980, and Norma Kamali adapted the weightlifter's outfit for aerobics.

Flares remained popular in the early seventies, and so elasticated cuffs inside skiing trousers were still useful. Motifs were essential: huge white snowballs printed on black, ski helmets painted with stars and stripes (custom painted motor-bike helmets were coveted until it was discovered that the paint weakened the structure of the helmet). Designer signatures began to be used both as status symbols and as surface decoration on all kinds of sportswear. 'Zipped-up technology' was vaunted: zip-off sleeves to transform a jacket into an instant gilet to wear with a piped slalom sweater. The sleeves could be made of parachute silk, wittily concertina-pleated in bright blue and turquoise so that movement revealed flashes of each colour. Gaiters were back in fashion and were made in the same concertina shape. Horizontal zips round the thigh, concealed by the stripes, made further divesting possible for summer. In the early seventies the essential accessories were polo-neck jumpers and fluffy skull caps, in the late seventies mirrored 'Easy Rider' sunglasses and headbands and, by the eighties, bikinis and the ubiquitous 'boogie pack'.

In the twenties removable layers and buckled-on drapes were essential for modesty's sake; in the eighties they were included for smartness. Popular features for cotton anoraks were down-filled zip-in linings and double-layered sleeves which peeled up and fastened at the shoulder to reveal a lighter and contrast-coloured sleeve underneath. Styles were borrowed from the thirties, too – in the seventies *Vogue* spotted a 1939 Charles James eiderdown-filled evening jacket in white satin which had been converted into a nylon and kapok ski jacket. By the early eighties the derivation was from the Mods of the sixties. Parkas were relaunched for the ski slopes and could double up as spring coats. For the speed conscious, fifties-style nylon trousers were worn, and for the expert, jeans; but for the rest, 'anti-glis' trousers padded and quilted at the knee and bottom guarded against bruises and dampness.

Blue 'sweat' anorak teamed with satin boxer shorts. BV 1980 Albert Watson. *Fiorucci, St Germain*

A futuristic silver, quilted helmet with a tinted visor for bright days on skis. GV 1980 Erwin Windmüller. *Penta-Sport*

As a reaction against the minuscule clothes of the sixties, designers and fabric manufacturers made an effort to expand their profits by producing garments made of huge amounts of material. The maxi advocated by *Vogue* as suitable for croquet was not a great success, but Oxford Bags for golf – worn with huge-lapelled, unstructured jackets, baker-boy hats and kipper ties – were objects of delight. These were all part of the tomboy look which was to blossom into the unisex trend. In 1980 German *Vogue* once again made an attempt to lever golf into the realms of fashion by advocating red bermudas and sweatshirts printed with palm trees and red and white two-tone shoes, but on the whole such efforts failed.

Teddy Tinling continued to design tennis wear with themes. In 1971 Evonne Goolagong wore a dress with an embroidered landscape of gum trees beside a creek. The vogue for headbands was so great at the end of the seventies that the Wimbledon committee had to permit coloured ones, but in 1983 Martina Navratilova was sent off at Wimbledon because her shirt was considered too bright. Gradually a new professionalism appeared, bringing clean lines, wrist bands and smart blue and red trims.

In times of recession fashion loses impetus and becomes derivative. In the early seventies elements of the forties styles were beginning to show and in 1980 street fashions even began to emulate imprisoning Edwardian clothes. Once again it took the influence of sportswear to release the wearer from such restrictions. There is now no place in sport for the cumbersome and impractical. Women have come so far that they no longer need to borrow men's clothes in order to assert their competence, but have taken them on as their own. The striking and angular clothes of the eighties accentuate wide shoulders 'capable of carrying the world'.

1980...

BV 1979 Mike Reinhardt. *Beged Or, Bombacha*

New, casual clothes for more leisure time developed into the 'land girl' look by the end of the seventies; clothes to be worn for fishing, rally driving, safaris, horse-riding or scrambling. The angler, *left*, has adopted the same policy as the keep fit fanatic, bored with traditional clothes, and is wearing pale blue suede. Rigidly traditional fabrics to suit each sport are no longer essential. The jeep driver, *opposite*, is wearing conventional camouflage fatigues but with one major difference – the hat and shirt are hand painted.

FV 1971 Helmut Newton. *Line Senghor*

BV 1971 Jonuelle. *The Scotch House (left), Jayne Swayne (centre), Sidney Smith (right)*

BV 1972 Clive Arrowsmith. *Lizzie Carr, Maudie Moon*

Fashion designers were using more fabric: the golfers, *opposite*, sport outfits which combine this trend with the new tomboy look: navy and white big check jackets, navy Oxford Bags, tweed caps and grey and white 'co-respondant' shoes. The sulky little boy to the left of the picture wears plaid knickerbockers. The romantic look popular in the early seventies influenced the two outfits, *above and right*. Both feature long languid lines and flared hemlines. The cotton and vincel tennis shirt has batwing sleeves, black neck and wrists and red buttons on the skirt. The golfer wears a lean lilac outfit in a linen, cotton and wool mixture.

BV 1972 Clive Arrowsmith. *Pringle*

More game-playing in the early seventies, *opposite*, when real sailor suits for sailing were the height of fashion. The mariner wears a piped sailor-collared shirt, stripey trousers and a white felt sailor hat with red stitching. A different and more constructive derivation is apparent, *right*. The source of this Norma Kamali leotard is the wrestling ring, and it is ideally suited for any kind of exercise or for weightlifting, the new women's sport.

BV 1983 Patrick Demarchelier. *Norma Kamali, Speedo, Joseph*

BV 1978 Alex Chatelain. *Slick Willies, Fiorucci*

By the late seventies, exercise was an obsession, with a whole range of clothes to cater for it. The sixties days when sportswear had to mould itself to the current fashion crazes were over; now sportswear was first in the race. The girl, *left*, is kitted out in a cotton and nylon tracksuit striped in blue, a white cotton singlet, running shoes and the latest fashion accessories: stopwatch, whistle and diving watch. The pastel pink satin vest and boxer shorts from Biba, *opposite right*, teamed with fuschia pink leather skating boots and the adored headband are suited to roller disco too. The exercise bike is another essential accessory, here accompanying a racy red and white tee shirt and shorts.

BV 1979 Albert Watson. *Biba, Walkers*

BV 1979 Albert Watson. *Cloo Cloo*

89

FV 1981 Gunter Sachs.
*Thierry Mugler, Tecnica
(below right: Philippe
Arnould/Descente)*

Slinky, elasticized
skiing trousers are
back, their tightness
emphasized by the
huge width of the
military-style
shoulders. This wedge
shape is achieved in all
four futuristic outfits,
opposite. Above left,
metallic polyester
anorak with podgy
rolls of fabric at neck
and wrists; *above right*,
metallic nylon jacket
which zips up in a V
shape, giving an
armoured breast-plate
effect. Stand-up collar
and military-style
epaulettes characterize
the jacket, *below left*.
Below right, salopettes
moulded to the body,
with reinforced inserts,
and windproof
salopettes with zip-off
sleeves which can be
craftily secreted
in a special pocket
inside. A striking
alternative to the
'interplanetary' look is
provided by the
'boogie pack' and
bathing suit worn by
the skier, *right*.

BV 1981 Uli Rose.
*Nelbarden, Sony,
Courtenay, Benetton,
The Scotch House,
Pindisports*

BV 1980 Bruno Juniner. *OMO Norma Kamali, Gamba, Paul Smith, Frieds*

The fanaticism with which dance and exercise have come to be regarded has led to ingenious attempts to deviate from the traditional leotard and tights. The dancer, *opposite*, wears a lycra top and matching flared skirt hung from a deep, plain basque. The weightlifter, *above*, with her dumb-bell, is kitted out in knickers with elasticated braces, lycra footless tights and soft leather jazz shoes. The girl ready for aerobics, *right*, wears an adaptation of the tracksuit, with flared shorts and button-front jacket.

IV 1981 Peter Ogilvie. *Trussardi*

93

The exhausted windsurfer, *right*, wears a wet suit composed of polyamide and polyurethane with reinforced knee pads and shoulder fasteners. Wet suits, first developed during the Second World War, are generally made of neoprene and nylon, but for a flashier, shinier suit, neoprene and lycra make a dazzling combination. Dry suits of Goretex (fabric which 'breathes') are the latest development: instead of accommodating a film of water inside the suit which warms up to the body's temperature, they keep the body absolutely dry and therefore much warmer.

FV 1982 Arnaud de Rosnay. *Ellesse*

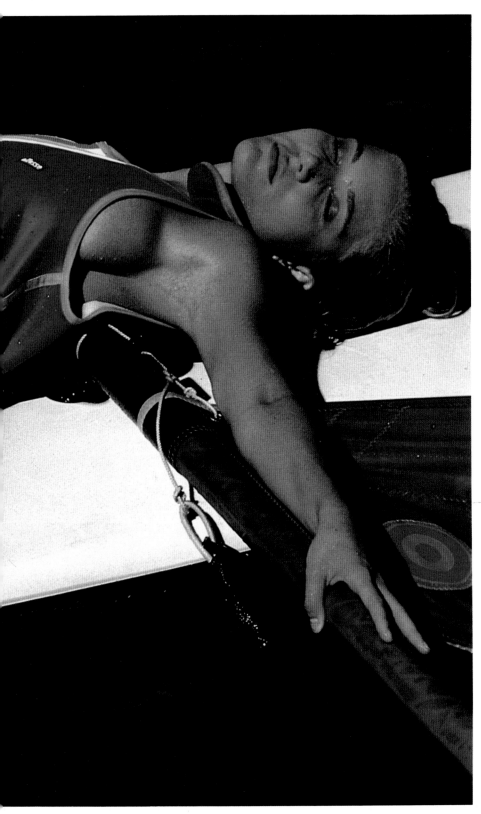

FV 1982 Arnaud de Rosnay. *Martini Sportline*

GV 1981 John Stember.

An alternative to the wet suit, *above*, for warmer days, is this overall of spinnaker material. It is light and airy with a huge puffy collar like a hood. For even warmer days, *top*, a front-zipping jersey costume is ideal.

A bodybuilder wearing a leotard and supportive weightlifter's belt. Bodybuilding has asserted not only women's strength, but their dedication to even the most gruelling sport. It is also a prime example of the supremacy of the body's dictates over restrictive fashion.

FV 1981 *Stacey Bentley photographed by Helmut Newton*